Dinner Parties

SIMPLE RECIPES FOR EASY ENTERTAINING

Jessica Strand

Photographs by Victoria Pearson

CHRONICLE BOOKS

SAN FRANCISCO

Text copyright © 2004 by Jessica Strand
Photographs copyright © 2004 by Victoria Pearson
All rights reserved. No part of this book may be
reproduced in any form without written permission
from the publisher.

Library of Congress Cataloging-in-Publication Data:
Strand, Jessica.
   Dinner parties : simple recipes for easy entertaining /
by Jessica Strand ; photographs by Victoria Pearson.
-- 1st ed.
        p. cm.
Includes index.
ISBN 0-8118-4298-3 (hardcover)
1 Dinners and dining. 2 Entertaining. 3 Menus. I. Title.
TX737.S882 2004
642'.4—dc22
                        2003019021

Manufactured in China.

Design: Carole Goodman / Blue Anchor Design

Prop stylist: Yolande Yorke-Edgell
Prop stylist's assistant: Nori Hubbs
Food stylist: Rori Trovato
Food stylist's assistant: Tina Wilson
Photographer's assistant: Jon Nakano

Distributed in Canada by Raincoast Books
9050 Shaughnessy Street
Vancouver, British Columbia V6P 6E5

10 9 8 7 6 5 4 3 2

Chronicle Books LLC
85 Second Street
San Francisco, California 94105

www.chroniclebooks.com

DEDICATION

To Stephen, who has helped to create, conceive, and consume the food for every divine, decadent dinner party I've ever given

ACKNOWLEDGMENTS

First of all, many thanks to my husband, Stephen, for his marvelous dessert recipes and for all his help and support. Thanks also to my dear, talented friend Tracy Scott, who not only tested many a recipe, but also meticulously proofed the manuscript. And, of course, this book would not exist without the brilliant, talented team at Chronicle Books, who make me look good time and time again. Thank you, Laurel Mainard, Carole Goodman, and Pamela Geismar. That group would not be complete without my lovely, thoughtful editor Leslie Jonath, who can lead a horse to water without ever getting it lost. A giant thanks to the immensely talented Victoria Pearson, whose beautiful photographs leave me speechless, but very hungry. And a thank-you to each and every friend who taste-tested my recipes and gave me frank, honest advice, praise, and criticism. And as always, thanks to my sweet bean, who patiently waits to play until after I've finished working. Thank you all.

TABLE OF CONTENTS

INTRODUCTION

FOR ME, GIVING A DINNER PARTY IS ONE OF LIFE'S GREAT pleasures. There's nothing like lingering at the table with friends after enjoying a luscious home-cooked meal. When I think of dinner parties at my home, I see candles nearly burned down to the end, lots of plates stacked in the sink, and my husband filling cordial glasses with port or limoncello.

There is something about giving a dinner party that jolts you out of your everyday routine and makes you focus on the evening ahead; like a vacation, you plan it with excitement. What will you serve? How many people will you have?

When I'm planning a dinner, my husband and I spend days deciding on the menu and the people we'd like to invite. Sometimes we end up having another couple over, while other times it could be a group of twelve. Whatever the size of the group, we excitedly page through cookbooks, reciting recipes aloud, gathering ideas for a menu. In my house, I do the main course and side dishes while my husband reigns in the kitchen when it comes to dessert.

In this book, I've divided the dinners by size, moving from intimate groups of four to bustling ones of ten to twelve. Doing so should make it easier for you to plan your own dinner party. The smaller dinners are a bit more elaborate, while the larger ones offer big dishes that are easy to serve to a crowd. When I use the word elaborate I don't mean "time intensive." On the contrary, the whole point of this book is help you create a dinner party in a relaxed, organized fashion so that you can really enjoy spending time with your guests.

Along with each menu is a Menu Manager that will allow you to plan your time most efficiently. The Menu Manager guides each step of the meal and helps you to prepare some dishes ahead of time. With the direction of the Menu Manager, not only will you have time before your company arrives, but time with your guests during the dinner.

When putting together the menus for this book, I made a list of all the dishes that have become "classics" in our household, like roasted asparagus with poached eggs, finished with a dusting of freshly grated Parmesan. Another is a tangy Andalusian gazpacho that will mystify your friends with its creamy texture; a few stale pieces of Italian bread give it body. I've included a recipe for a succulent herb-marinated pork shoulder that quickly became a standard at my house; I must have cooked it at least six times over last winter and spring. I've also included my husband's blueberry pie, which is easy to assemble and always has purple-lipped dinner guests begging for more.

Whatever its size, a dinner party is about sharing food and enjoying each other's company. Friends usually like to lend a hand at these events, whether clearing the table, tossing a salad, or serving dessert. The best kind of dinner party has a relaxed, communal air where everyone is involved, even if it's just sitting and chatting with each other.

A friend once told me that if the hosts of a party are having fun, then everyone else will have fun, too. This comment certainly applies to dinner parties. You can have the best food, the best wine, and a beautiful setting, but if you're stressed and miserable, your guests will feel it. So first and foremost, have a wonderful time, and all the rest will follow.

DINNER PARTY PLANNING TIPS

- Take your time. Have fun setting up your apartment or house for the party.

- Try to have your house and table ready at least 1 hour before your guests arrive. As for the food, the main dishes should be ready or under way, and the rest should be ready to assemble without much thought.

- Think through your music choices before a dinner party begins. You don't want to be fumbling through CDs while your guests are arriving or during dinner.

- Always have ice on hand for drinks, water, and so on.

- Always have bottled water on hand, both still and sparkling. Also, make sure to have extra mixers and fruit juices for people who want something nonalcoholic.

- Make an effort to introduce your guests to each other, finding the common thread between them. It seems old-fashioned, but it's one of the keys to having your guests enjoy themselves.

- Always buy more wine than you think you'll need. You never want to run out during a dinner party.

- Give yourself enough time to bring meat to room temperature.

- You can prepare your salad dressing days ahead of time. Just remember to let it come to room temperature for an hour or two before dressing the salad.

- Salads can be composed without dressing and without nuts hours ahead of time; just remember to cover them with plastic wrap.

- People feel welcome when you treat them to a special cocktail, glass of wine, or delectable nosh after your initial greeting.

- Careful planning allows you to purchase many items well ahead of time, like ice, wine, water, and many of the ingredients for desserts. As for vegetables, meat, and fish, they should be purchased right before the party.

- Remember that large centerpieces make it difficult for guests to converse. The same often can be said for large candles or candelabra. Short candles or votives are a good alternative.

- Keep things simple and organized, and you will be guaranteed a fun-filled, stress-free dinner party.

DINNERS FOR FOUR

INTIMATE DINNERS

A DINNER FOR FOUR IS AN INTIMATE, COZY AFFAIR WHERE YOU are certain to spend time talking to your guests. It's an event that quietly says, "I'd like to spend quality time with you." With such a small group, you can be more ambitious with your courses since it will be easy to pace the evening's menu. Because the size is so manageable, it's easy to prepare individual dishes like tartlets or chocolate sundaes, which always make your guests feel special.

A SOUTHERN DINNER
WITH A TWIST

Lillet Cocktail

Dry Rub Pork Ribs

Asian Coleslaw

Corn on the Cob with Whipped Parsley Butter

Chocolate Sundaes

MENU MANAGER

2 days before dinner:	Prepare chocolate sauce
1 day before dinner:	Prepare vanilla ice cream
Morning of dinner:	Prepare Asian slaw and parsley butter
2½ hours before dinner:	Prepare rub for pork ribs
2 hours before dinner:	Prepare or heat grill and begin cooking ribs
1 hour before dinner:	Shuck corn
30 minutes before dinner:	Put water and corn on stove
When guests arrive:	Prepare cocktails

Lillet Cocktail

If you've never tasted Lillet, you're in for a treat. It's been made in the village of Podensac, a few miles south of Bordeaux in southwest France, since 1887, and is readily available in many liquor stores. A fortified wine blended with a special combination of fruits and herbs, it is a classic aperitif. It's divine served over ice with a slice of orange.

SERVES 1

3 ounces Lillet

ice cubes

1 orange slice

soda water (optional)

Pour the Lillet into a red-wine glass half-filled with ice. Garnish with the orange slice. Add soda water to taste if using.

Dry Rub Pork Ribs

The secret to this recipe is using baby back ribs rather than spare ribs. Baby backs come from the back of the pig, where the meat is more tender, plus their small size makes it easier to grill them in a shorter period of time. And the best part here is the use of a sweet and spicy dry rub, which beats any barbecue sauce you've ever tasted.

SERVES 4

DRY RUB:
1½ tablespoons freshly ground pepper

2½ tablespoons chili powder

¼ cup sweet Hungarian paprika

2 tablespoons sea salt

5 tablespoons sugar

2 tablespoons ground cumin

2 slabs of baby back pork ribs (approximately 3 to 3½ pounds)

To prepare the dry rub: In a medium bowl, combine all the dry rub ingredients. Stir to blend well.

Rinse the ribs and pat dry with paper towels. Thoroughly rub the ribs on both sides with the dry rub.

Build a small fire on one side of a charcoal grill with a cover, or preheat half of a gas grill to medium. Place the ribs on the grill. Cover the grill and partially close the vents. Cook for 45 minutes. Replenish the charcoal fire with fresh coals. Flip the ribs and cook for another 45 minutes, or until tender.

Asian Coleslaw

My guests are crazy about this simple Asian slaw. Its light, clean taste makes it a wonderful accompaniment to the spicy, rich pork ribs. It also works well with most grilled meats or fish.

SERVES 4

3 tablespoons white sesame seeds

½ green cabbage, cored and cut into ¼-inch-thick lengthwise slices

½ red cabbage, cored and cut into ¼-inch-thick lengthwise slices

1 carrot, peeled and shredded

2 green onions, white part only, thinly sliced

½ cup minced fresh cilantro

DRESSING:

1 clove garlic, minced

1 tablespoon minced fresh ginger

2 tablespoons hoisin sauce

¼ cup canola oil

2 tablespoons Asian sesame oil

3 tablespoons rice vinegar

Preheat the oven to 400°F. Spread the sesame seeds in a pie pan and toast in the oven until they are golden, 3 to 4 minutes. Keep your eye on them since they can go from golden to black quickly. Remove from the oven and set aside.

In a large bowl, combine the cabbage, carrot, green onions, and cilantro.

To prepare the dressing: In a small bowl, combine all the dressing ingredients and whisk until thoroughly blended.

Pour the dressing over the slaw. Toss until completely coated. Sprinkle the slaw with the toasted sesame seeds and toss again. Let the slaw stand at room temperature for at least 30 minutes before serving.

Corn on the Cob with Whipped Parsley Butter

My mother-in-law introduced me to this foolproof method of cooking corn that is still crisp and never soggy. The parsley butter adds a special touch.

SERVES 4

½ cup (1 stick) unsalted butter at room temperature

3 tablespoons minced fresh flat-leaf parsley

6 ears corn (so you have a little extra in case people want seconds), shucked and rinsed

In a medium bowl, combine the butter and parsley. Whip together with a whisk or electric mixer until completely blended. Return to the refrigerator for at least 1 hour to set.

Fill a large stockpot with water and let it come to room temperature. Add the corn and set the pan over medium-high heat, uncovered. When the water just begins to boil, the corn is done. If you're not ready to serve the corn, cover the pot and move it to a cool burner. The corn will remain perfectly cooked for another 10 to 15 minutes, but after that it will become overcooked.

Using a melon baller or a teaspoon, scoop 2 to 3 balls of butter and place them on each plate. Serve the corn next to the butter.

Chocolate Sundaes

The use of Mexican chocolate in the sauce gives this classic dessert a special taste. Find the best vanilla bean available to make the ice cream, and make sure to scrape every last seed from the bean before removing it from the mixture.

MAKES 1 QUART ICE CREAM; SERVES 4

VANILLA BEAN ICE CREAM:
1½ cups whole milk

1 vanilla bean, split lengthwise

¾ cup sugar

⅛ teaspoon salt

2 egg yolks

2 cups heavy cream

CHOCOLATE SAUCE:
9 ounces Mexican chocolate, chopped

½ cup water

¼ cup heavy cream

1 tablespoon Kahlúa liqueur

To prepare the ice cream: In a medium saucepan, heat the milk over low heat until bubbles form around the edges of the pan. Scrape the seeds from the vanilla bean into the milk. Add the bean to the pan. Stir the milk for 1 to 2 minutes. Stir in the sugar and salt until dissolved. Remove from heat and let cool for 10 minutes.

In a small stainless-steel bowl, beat the egg yolks until blended. Gradually whisk in the milk mixture until combined. Remove the vanilla bean. Set the bowl over a saucepan of barely simmering water. Cook, stirring constantly, for 10 to 12 minutes, or until the mixture is thick enough to coat the back of the spoon. Remove from the heat and let cool. Stir in the cream.

Cover and refrigerate for at least 3 hours. Freeze in an ice cream maker according to the manufacturer's instructions.

To prepare the chocolate sauce: In a double boiler over barely simmering water, combine the chocolate and water and stir until the chocolate is melted and the sauce begins to thicken.

Remove from heat and add the cream and Kahlúa. Stir until well combined.

Let cool and serve, or store in an airtight jar in the refrigerator for up to 2 weeks.

To serve, place a scoop of ice cream in each of 4 shallow bowls and either top with the chocolate sauce or serve the chocolate sauce in a small pitcher for your guests to add as they like.

AN ELEGANT STEAK FEAST

Leek and Potato Soup

Roasted Beet, Mâche, Gorgonzola, and Toasted Walnut Salad

Grilled Rib-Eye Steaks with Salsa Verde

Garlic Bread

Lemon-Rosemary Sorbet

MENU MANAGER

2 days before dinner:	Prepare salsa verde
1 day before dinner:	Prepare soup Prepare sorbet Prepare salad dressing
Morning of dinner:	Roast the beets Roast the walnuts
1 hour before dinner:	Prepare garlic bread up to heating Assemble salad without dressing
45 to 30 minutes before dinner:	Prepare grill for steaks Preheat oven for garlic bread
15 minutes before dinner:	Heat garlic bread
5 minutes before dinner:	Grill steaks Dress salad

Leek and Potato Soup

This soup is smooth, silky, and simple. And if that's not enough, it can be eaten either hot or cold. Using equal parts leeks and potatoes gives the mild potatoes a sweet, buttery taste. For a luxurious garnish, drizzle a little truffle oil on top.

SERVES 4

2 tablespoons unsalted butter

3 large leeks, white part only, well washed, trimmed, and quartered crosswise

3 large potatoes, peeled and quartered

3 cups chicken stock

3 ½ cups water

½ cup heavy cream

Sea salt and freshly ground pepper to taste

Juice of ½ lemon

4 teaspoons minced fresh chives for garnish

In a medium saucepan, melt the butter over medium heat. Add the leeks and sauté until they begin to soften, about 15 minutes. Remove from the heat and set aside.

In a medium stockpot, combine the leeks, potatoes, stock, and 3 cups of the water. Bring to a boil over high heat. Reduce the heat to low and simmer until the vegetables are soft, about 45 minutes.

In a blender or food processor, purée the soup in batches until smooth.

Return the soup to the stockpot and reheat. Stir in the cream, the remaining ½ cup water, salt, and pepper. Whisk in the lemon juice.

Divide among 4 bowls. Garnish each bowl with 1 teaspoon of chives.

Vichyssoise: Let the above soup cool and refrigerate for 2 hours or more. Dilute the soup with ½ cup water before serving.

Roasted Beet, Mâche, Gorgonzola, and Toasted Walnut Salad

This favorite salad is not only beautiful, it's sweet and salty, crunchy and soft. Mâche is a unique, delicate green with a subtle, sweet flavor. It has recently become more readily available at farmers' markets, specialty markets, and many grocery stores across the country. If you can't find mâche, substitute watercress.

SERVES 4

2 each golf-ball-sized golden and red beets

½ cup walnut halves

4 cups mâche

3 tablespoons crumbled Italian Gorgonzola cheese

VINAIGRETTE:
1 clove garlic, minced

¾ teaspoon Dijon mustard

Pinch of sugar

Sea salt and freshly ground pepper to taste

4 teaspoons sherry vinegar

2 teaspoons fresh lemon juice

⅓ cup olive oil

Preheat the oven to 400°F.

Cut the beet greens off, leaving ½ inch of the stems. Wash the beets and place in a small roasting pan. Bake for 50 minutes, or until tender. Let cool.

Peel the beets. Cut each beet into quarters and set aside.

Spread the walnuts on a pie plate and toast in the oven until golden brown, 3 to 5 minutes. Remove from the oven and set aside.

In a large bowl, combine the beets and mâche. Sprinkle with the toasted nuts and Gorgonzola.

To prepare the vinaigrette: In a small bowl, combine the garlic, mustard, sugar, salt, and pepper. Whisk in the vinegar and lemon juice. Gradually whisk in the olive oil to make an emulsified dressing.

Before serving, whisk the vinaigrette again and sprinkle over the salad. Toss until all the ingredients are coated and serve.

Grilled Rib-Eye Steaks with Salsa Verde

A juicy steak served with a generous pool of this herbal citrus sauce is as simple to prepare as it is elegant to serve. You can make the sauce the night before and let the flavors meld overnight. Remember to use the freshest herbs you can find.

SERVES 4

4 (8-ounce) boneless rib-eye (Spencer) steaks

2 tablespoons olive oil

2 tablespoons sea salt

Freshly ground pepper to taste

Salsa Verde (page 30) for serving

Light a fire in a charcoal grill or preheat a gas grill to medium-high. Rub the steaks with the olive oil and season with the salt and pepper.

Place the steaks on the grill rack and grill for 4 to 5 minutes on each side for medium-rare. (To check the doneness, use a sharp knife to cut into one of the steaks; the meat should be juicy and pink.)

Slice each steak and serve on a warmed plate with 3 generous spoonfuls of salsa verde on the side.

(continued)

Lemon-Rosemary Sorbet

You may be thinking to yourself: "Rosemary in lemon sorbet?" But it's simply delicious. The herb is steeped in simple syrup, then strained to add its buttery herbal taste to the tart lemon flavor, making this a refreshing palate pleaser.

MAKES 1 ½ PINTS

1 ½ cups sugar

1 ½ cups water

⅓ to ½ cup minced fresh rosemary

1 ⅓ cups fresh lemon juice

3 tablespoons vodka (optional)

In a medium saucepan, combine the sugar and water. Set over high heat and cook, stirring occasionally, until the sugar is completely dissolved and the syrup is simmering, about 5 minutes. Remove from heat.

Add the rosemary, lemon juice, and vodka (if using) to the syrup. Stir well. Let cool to room temperature, then refrigerate for at least 2 hours.

Strain the syrup through cheesecloth, then freeze in an ice cream maker according to the manufacturer's instructions.

A RUSTIC
VEGETARIAN DINNER

**Roasted Asparagus with Poached Eggs
and Parmesan Cheese**

Savory Caramelized Onion, Tomato, and Basil Tart

**Watercress and Roasted-Shallot Salad
with Tangerine Vinaigrette**

Peachy Cream Rustic Tartlets

MENU MANAGER

1 day before dinner: Prepare savory tart crust

Morning of dinner: Caramelize onions and set aside
Roast shallots
Prepare tangerine vinaigrette

4 hours before dinner: Prepare shortbread tart disks
Prepare remaining dessert components

1 hour before dinner: Roast asparagus
Assemble salad without dressing

10 minutes before dinner: Prepare poached eggs

Roasted Asparagus with Poached Eggs and Parmesan Cheese

In my family, we make this dish for dinner at least once a week. I call it "asparagus with poor man's hollandaise." Once you pierce that rich, runny yolk and dip your smoky roasted asparagus into it, you'll wonder why you ever made hollandaise at all.

SERVES 4

2 bunches asparagus, trimmed

3 tablespoons olive oil

Sea salt and freshly ground pepper

½ teaspoon red pepper flakes

3 tablespoons white wine or rice vinegar

4 eggs

4 tablespoons freshly grated Parmesan cheese

Preheat the broiler.

Spread the asparagus on a baking sheet or two (depending on the size of the stalks) without crowding them. Drizzle the asparagus with the olive oil, then roll them in the oil to coat the stalks. Sprinkle with the salt, pepper, and red pepper flakes.

Roast the asparagus, turning them once, for 12 to 15 minutes, or until crisp-tender and lightly browned.

Add 3 inches of water to a large skillet and place over medium heat until the water comes to a low simmer. Add the vinegar. Wait for 1 minute, then add the eggs by cracking each into a saucer and carefully slipping the egg into the water. Let the eggs cook for 4 minutes. If the yolks still look too runny for your liking, spoon water on top of the eggs and cook another 30 seconds. Remove the eggs carefully from the water with a slotted spoon.

Divide the asparagus among 4 warmed plates. Put a poached egg on top of each bundle. Sprinkle each egg with 1 tablespoon of the Parmesan cheese and serve immediately.

Savory Caramelized Onion, Tomato, and Basil Tart

This recipe uses ingredients that are most delicious in summer, but it can change with the season. In the spring, you could use asparagus; in the winter, thinly sliced potatoes with onions and olives; and in fall, figs and prosciutto. Use flat-leaf parsley when basil is not available. The crust has a touch of cornmeal to give it a slightly crunchy texture.

SERVES 4

CRUST:
1¼ cups all-purpose flour

⅓ cup fine yellow cornmeal

1½ teaspoons sea salt

1 teaspoon sugar

6 tablespoons cold unsalted butter, cut into 6 pieces

¼ cup ice water

3 tablespoons olive oil

TOPPING:
5 tablespoons olive oil

3 yellow onions, halved and thinly sliced crosswise

Sea salt and freshly ground pepper to taste

4 cloves garlic, thinly sliced

3 large very ripe tomatoes, halved, seeded, and thinly sliced

10 niçoise olives, halved and pitted

1 large egg yolk beaten with 1 teaspoon milk

½ cup coarsely chopped fresh basil

To prepare the crust: In a food processor, combine the flour, cornmeal, salt, and sugar. Pulse briefly to combine. Add the butter and pulse until the mixture resembles coarse crumbs, 5 to 10 seconds but no longer. Add the water and olive oil and pulse 15 to 20 times, or until the dough just begins to hold together. Transfer to a lightly floured surface and flatten into a round disk. Cover in plastic wrap and refrigerate for at least 1 hour or up to 2 days.

To start the topping: In a medium skillet, heat the olive oil over medium heat, then add the onions. Cook, stirring frequently, until lightly browned,

(continued)

soft, and translucent, 25 to 30 minutes. As they cook, season with salt and pepper. After about 20 minutes, or when most of the onions appear just about done, add the garlic and cook along with the onions. Remove from heat and let cool.

To assemble the tart: Preheat the oven to 375°F. Line a baking sheet with parchment paper.

On a lightly floured surface, roll the dough out to a 15-inch round. Lift the sides with a spatula as you roll and spread flour underneath to avoid sticking. Transfer the dough by rolling it around the rolling pin and unrolling it on the lined baking sheet.

Spread the onions and garlic over the dough, leaving a 2-inch border. Arrange the tomato slices in a single layer over the top, then sprinkle the olives evenly over the onion-garlic mixture and tomatoes. Sprinkle with the salt and pepper.

Fold the edge of dough over the filling, pleating as you go. Brush the egg yolk mixture over the rim.

Bake for 30 minutes, or until the crust is golden. Remove from the oven and let cool on a wire rack for 10 to 15 minutes. Serve immediately, or let cool to room temperature before serving. In either case, sprinkle the tart with the chopped basil just before serving.

Watercress and Roasted-Shallot Salad with Tangerine Vinaigrette

This peppery green salad tossed with a tangy tangerine dressing is satisfying enough to serve as a main dish with a good loaf of bread, a glass of wine, and a delicious nutty cheese. If tangerines aren't available, use oranges.

SERVES 4

16 small shallots

3 tablespoons olive oil

4 bunches watercress, stemmed
   (about 5 cups)

DRESSING:

1 teaspoon Dijon mustard

¼ cup fresh tangerine juice

1 tablespoon balsamic vinegar

½ cup olive oil

1½ teaspoons minced fresh thyme

Sea salt and freshly ground pepper
   to taste

Preheat the oven to 350°F.

Toss the shallots in the olive oil to coat them. Spread the shallots on a baking sheet and roast for 1 hour, or until golden and very soft.

Put the watercress in a large salad bowl.

To prepare the dressing: In a medium bowl, combine the mustard, tangerine juice, and vinegar. Gradually whisk in the olive oil to make an emulsified sauce. Whisk in the thyme, salt, and pepper.

Pour the vinaigrette over the watercress and toss until coated.

Divide the greens among 4 plates and arrange 4 roasted shallots on top of each serving.

Peachy Cream Rustic Tartlets

I first tasted a tart similar to these at Empire Restaurant in Providence, Rhode Island. I've made some changes to the recipe over the years and sometimes substitute nectarines. But for me, there's nothing like that perfect peach.

MAKES 4 INDIVIDUAL TARTS

SHORTBREAD PASTRY:
1 cup all-purpose flour

¼ cup granulated sugar

½ cup (1 stick) cold unsalted
    butter, cut into small pieces

PEACH FILLING:
4 peaches (about 2¼ pounds),
    peeled, pitted, and cut into
    ½-inch-thick slices

⅓ cup granulated sugar

CANDIED PECANS:
⅔ cup pecans, coarsely chopped

4 teaspoons packed brown sugar

2½ tablespoons unsalted butter,
    cut into small pieces

¼ teaspoon salt

WHIPPED CREAM:
1½ cups heavy cream

1½ tablespoons confectioners'
    sugar, sifted

Confectioners' sugar for dusting

Preheat the oven to 375°F.

   To prepare the pastry: In a food processor, pulse the flour and sugar together. Add the butter, pulsing until the mixture forms a crumbly dough, 15 to 20 seconds. On a lightly floured surface, form into a ball and cut into quarters. Roll each piece between 2 pieces of waxed paper to make a 4-inch-diameter round about ¼ inch thick. Remove the top piece of paper and cut the pastry into a perfect 3½-inch-diameter round using a biscuit or cookie cutter. Invert the rounds onto an ungreased baking sheet and carefully remove the remaining sheet of waxed paper.

   Bake for 12 to 15 minutes, or until golden brown. Transfer to a wire rack and let cool.

   To prepare the filling: Preheat the oven to 375°F, if necessary. Butter a baking sheet.

(continued)

Spread the peaches on the prepared sheet and sprinkle with the sugar. Roast for 15 to 20 minutes, or until the peaches are soft and browned on the edges. Remove from the oven and let cool.

To prepare the candied pecans: Preheat the oven to 275°F.

Spread the pecans on a baking sheet and sprinkle with the brown sugar, butter, and salt. Bake, stirring occasionally with a long spoon to avoid burning, for 12 to 15 minutes, or until the nuts are a deep amber brown in color.

To prepare the whipped cream: In a deep bowl, using an electric mixer, whip the cream with the confectioners' sugar until soft peaks form. Cover and refrigerate for up to 2 hours. Whisk a few times before using.

To serve, place each shortbread round on a plate and top with one-fourth of the peaches and one-fourth of the whipped cream. Sprinkle with one-fourth of the candied pecans and dust with confectioners' sugar.

DINNERS FOR SIX

FULL OF CONVERSATION

WITH SIX GUESTS, THE DYNAMIC QUICKLY CHANGES. THERE'S MORE talk and a bit more noise, and though the dinner remains intimate, the conversations are more varied. People have a tendency to break into smaller groups and chat. When it comes to food, six is probably the easiest number to cook for: you can choose to serve several courses or a one-pot meal, or a roast, and either one large or individual desserts. That's why I've included an array of dishes, from Sicilian pasta to beef stew to lamb chops. For desserts, there's a delectable Raspberry Tart, individual old-fashioned buttery short-cakes with fresh strawberries and whipped cream, and a Key Lime Pie.

A TOUCH OF SICILY

Sicilian Sardine Pasta

Roasted Sweet-and-Sour Orange Chicken

Arugula and Endive Salad

Raspberry Tart

MENU MANAGER

Morning of dinner:	Prepare raspberry tart Prepare salad dressing
1½ hours before dinner:	Prepare chicken
1 hour before dinner:	Prepare Sicilian pasta sauce Assemble salad; cover with plastic wrap and refrigerate
15 minutes before dinner:	Put pasta water on stove

Sicilian Sardine Pasta

Whenever I tell my mother I've made this pasta for a dinner party she invariably says, "You mean the Sicilian pasta," and I respond, "Yes, the one with the sardines, pine nuts, and currants." Apparently, this pasta is a favorite in Sicily, as well as at my house. You could use fresh sardines for this recipe (you'll need about 1 pound, filleted), but it's just as good with canned.

SERVES 6

5 tablespoons dried currants or raisins

1 fennel bulb, trimmed (fronds reserved)

2 (3¾-ounce) cans oil-packed sardines

3 tablespoons olive oil

1 teaspoon red pepper flakes

4 slices crusty baguette, cut into ½-inch dice

1 yellow onion, chopped

⅓ cup pine nuts

4 anchovies, chopped

1½ pounds dried shaped pasta, such as farfalle or fusilli

Soak the currants or raisins in hot water for 20 minutes until plump; drain and set aside.

Chop the fennel bulb and mince the fennel fronds. Reserve 2 or 3 tablespoons of the fronds for garnish.

Drain the oil from the sardine cans into a large saucepan or sauté pan. Add 1 tablespoon of the olive oil. Heat the oil over medium heat. Add the red pepper flakes and the remaining minced fennel fronds. Sauté for 1 minute.

Add the diced bread to the pan and sauté for 3 to 5 minutes, or until golden and crisp. Using a slotted spoon, transfer to paper towels to drain.

Add the remaining 2 tablespoons olive oil to the saucepan and heat over medium heat. Add the onion and chopped fennel bulb and sauté for 10 minutes, or until soft. Add the pine nuts, anchovies, and currants. Sauté for 3 minutes. Turn off the heat.

(continued)

In a large pot of salted boiling water, cook the pasta until tender but still firm to the bite, about 10 minutes.

Meanwhile, add the sardines to the saucepan and break them up with a wooden spoon. Sauté over medium heat for 5 minutes. Add the croutons and sauté for 2 minutes. Turn off the heat.

Drain the pasta, then transfer to the saucepan and toss with the sauce.

Serve in warmed shallow bowls, garnished with a dusting of the reserved fennel fronds.

Roasted Sweet-and-Sour Orange Chicken

A dish I ate years ago at a Mexican restaurant inspired this recipe. The orange and kumquats add a sweet-and-sour citrus flavor to the meat, while the thyme embues it with an earthy aromatic flavor. You'll find kumquats in season from the beginning of winter until early spring.

SERVES 6

2 chickens, 3½ pounds each

Sea salt

8 kumquats

2 large oranges

10 to 12 sprigs fresh thyme, each about 3 inches long

4 tablespoons olive oil

Preheat the oven to 425°F. Remove the giblets from the chickens and reserve for another use. Rinse the chickens inside and out. Pat dry with paper towels. Salt the body cavities liberally. Roll the kumquats between your hands to soften. Stuff 4 kumquats into each body cavity and follow with an orange. Loosen the skin over the breast of each chicken and place 5 to 6 thyme sprigs under the surface of the skin, running lengthwise. Rub each bird with 2 tablespoons of the olive oil.

Place the chickens, breast side up, on a roasting rack in a roasting pan. Roast for about 1¼ hours, or until an instant read thermometer inserted in the thickest part of the thigh and not touching the bone registers 170°F, or the juices run clear when the thigh is pierced.

Remove the chickens from the oven. Transfer to a cutting board and cover them loosely with aluminum foil. Let rest for 10 minutes, then carve and serve.

Arugula and Endive Salad

This simple salad has so much flavor that all it needs is a light dressing. Make sure the arugula is fresh. There's nothing worse than a wizened peppery green.

SERVES 6

1 bunch arugula, stemmed

5 Belgian endives, cut crosswise
  into ¼-inch-thick slices

DRESSING:

5 tablespoons olive oil

Juice of ½ lemon

1 tablespoon cider vinegar

1 clove garlic, minced

Pinch of sugar

Sea salt and freshly ground pepper
  to taste

Put the greens in a large salad bowl.

   To prepare the dressing: In a small bowl, whisk all the dressing ingredients together. Taste and adjust the seasoning.

   Toss the salad with the dressing until all the leaves are lightly coated.

Raspberry Tart

This tart is loosely based on one Patricia Wells included in her book *Bistro Cooking*. Like many of the tarts in French bistros, it's simple yet elegant, and the perfect finish to any meal. Over the years, I've changed the ingredients slightly to suit my taste, but it's not far from one served at *Le Jura* café in Lyon. Make this tart the day you plan to serve it.

MAKES ONE 10 1/2-INCH TART; SERVES 6 TO 8

PASTRY:

1 cup all-purpose flour

6 tablespoons cold unsalted
    butter, cut into pieces

⅛ teaspoon salt

½ cup confectioners' sugar

1 large egg, beaten

FILLING:

3 large egg yolks

¾ cup crème fraîche

3½ tablespoons granulated sugar

2 cups fresh raspberries

Confectioners' sugar for dusting

To prepare the pastry: In a food processor, combine the flour, butter, salt, and sugar. Pulse until the mixture resembles coarse crumbs, 5 to 10 seconds but no longer. Add the egg and pulse 15 to 20 times, or until the pastry just begins to hold together. Transfer to waxed paper and flatten into a 10-inch-diameter disk.

Using your fingertips lightly dusted with flour, press the disk into a 10½-inch false-bottomed tart pan. Working quickly, press the dough along the bottom and up the sides. Run a rolling pin over the top of the pan to trim the dough. Cover with plastic wrap and refrigerate for 1½ to 2 hours.

Preheat the oven to 350°F.

Prick the bottom of the tart shell with a fork and line it with aluminum foil, pressing into all the edges to avoid shrinkage while baking. Fill with pie weights or dried beans. Bake just until the pastry begins to brown on the edges, about 20 minutes. Remove the weights and foil and return shell to the oven for 15 to 20 minutes, or until uniformly browned. Watch carefully after 10 minutes, because this crust can go from browned to burned very quickly. Let cool on a wire rack for at least 20 minutes.

(continued)

To prepare the filling: Preheat the oven to 375°F.

In a medium bowl, beat the egg yolks until blended then add the crème fraîche and sugar. Stir until blended, then pour into the pastry shell.

Arrange the berries in a single layer on top of the filling.

Carefully place in the center of the oven and bake for about 15 minutes, or until the filling begins to set. Let cool completely on a wire rack before serving. Dust with confectioners' sugar.

FIRST-SIGNS-OF-SPRING FEAST

Manchego Cheese, Dates, and Pistachios

Grilled Lamb Chops with Roasted Grape, Olive, and Walnut Relish

Brussels Sprouts Hash

Strawberry Shortcakes

MENU MANAGER

Morning of dinner:	Prepare shortcakes
2 hours before dinner:	Prepare strawberries Prepare grape, olive, and walnut relish
1 hour before dinner:	Bring lamb chops to room temperature Prepare Brussels sprouts hash Prepare whipped cream
45 minutes before dinner:	Prepare or preheat grill
30 minutes before dinner:	Assemble cheese, nuts, and dates
10 minutes before dinner:	Place lamb chops on grill Reheat Brussels sprouts hash

Manchego Cheese, Dates, and Pistachios

In the last several years, the Spanish cheese Manchego has become widely available. This subtle dry cheese pairs beautifully with dried fruits and nuts for a sophisticated beginning to your meal. Serve with Campari and soda with a twist of lime, or a nice, velvety Pinot Noir.

SERVES 6

1 wedge Manchego cheese (about 1 pound)

12 large, plump dates, halved and pitted

1 cup salted pistachios

On a platter, arrange the wedge of cheese, the dates, and a small bowl of the nuts.

Grilled Lamb Chops with Roasted Grape, Olive, and Walnut Relish

Though lamb chops are a bit pricey, there's really nothing like them for a dinner party: they're easy to cook and eat. A simple coating of olive oil, salt, and pepper is all that's needed, but feel free to rub both sides with Dijon mustard and some minced fresh rosemary, if you prefer.

SERVES 6

12 lamb chops, each 1 inch thick

2 tablespoons olive oil

1½ tablespoons sea salt

1½ tablespoons freshly ground pepper

Roasted Grape, Olive, and Walnut Relish (recipe follows) for serving

Prepare a fire in a charcoal grill or preheat a gas grill to medium-high. Rub the chops with olive oil and sprinkle with the salt and pepper.

Place the chops on the grill rack and cook for 4 to 6 minutes on each side for medium-rare. (Use a sharp knife to cut into one of the chops; the meat should be juicy and pink.)

Serve with the relish.

ROASTED GRAPE, OLIVE, AND WALNUT RELISH

SERVES 6

3 cups mixed seedless grapes (black, Red Flame, or green)

1½ cups walnut halves

2 cups picholine, niçoise, or black oil-cured olives, pitted

3 tablespoons aged balsamic vinegar

1½ tablespoons olive oil

5 sprigs fresh thyme

Preheat the oven to 350°F. In an ovenproof dish, combine all the ingredients. Bake, uncovered, for 45 minutes, stirring occasionally. Serve warm.

Brussels Sprouts Hash

This could make you a convert if you've never been a fan of Brussels sprouts, and if you've always adored them, you'll be happy to add this recipe to your repertoire.

SERVES 6

½ cup walnuts, coarsely chopped

5 tablespoons olive oil

1½ small yellow onions, finely chopped

4 cloves garlic, thinly sliced diagonally

2 pounds Brussels sprouts, cut into ⅛-inch-thick crosswise slices

4 cups chicken stock

Sea salt and freshly ground pepper to taste

½ cup freshly grated Parmesan cheese

3 tablespoons coarsely chopped fresh flat-leaf parsley

Preheat the oven to 375°F. In a pie tin, spread the chopped walnuts. Toast in the oven for 5 to 7 minutes, or until golden brown. Set aside.

In a large saucepan, heat the olive oil over medium heat. Add the onions and garlic and sauté for 4 to 5 minutes, or until the onions begin to soften and turn golden. Make sure not to let the garlic burn, or it will be bitter.

Add the Brussels sprouts to the pan and sauté for 15 minutes, or until lightly browned, gradually adding 2 cups of the stock as needed to keep the mixture from scorching. Cook uncovered for another 8 to 10 minutes, gradually stirring in the remaining 2 cups stock, until the greens are wilted and slightly golden on the edges. Cook a few minutes longer, until lightly browned and crisp. Season with the salt and pepper.

To serve, spread the hash on a small platter. Sprinkle with the walnuts, Parmesan cheese, and parsley.

Strawberry Shortcakes

This simple combination of fresh strawberries, whipped cream, and home-baked shortcakes never seems to disappoint. Take a few moments to make the short-cakes from scratch and use the best strawberries possible, and you'll be amazed at how easily this classic comes together.

MAKES 6 INDIVIDUAL SHORTCAKES

2 cups all-purpose flour

2 tablespoons plus 1 teaspoon
   granulated sugar

1 tablespoon baking powder

¼ teaspoon salt

½ cup (1 stick) cold unsalted
   butter, cut into small pieces

1 egg

¼ cup buttermilk

¼ cup heavy cream

4 pints fresh strawberries, hulled

4 tablespoons sifted confectioners'
   sugar, plus more for dusting

2 cups heavy cream

3 tablespoons Cointreau or other
   orange liqueur

Preheat the oven to 400°F. Adjust an oven rack in the lower third of the oven. Grease a baking sheet.

In a food processor, combine the flour, sugar, baking powder, and salt. Pulse for a few seconds to mix the ingredients. Add the butter and pulse until the mixture resembles coarse crumbs, 5 to 10 seconds but no longer. In a small bowl, combine the egg, buttermilk, and cream. Whisk to blend and add to the food processor. Pulse for 5 to 10 times, or until the pastry just begins to hold together. Be careful not to overblend at this point.

Place the dough on a floured work surface and knead it 5 to 6 times, just until the dough comes together completely. Roll into a round about 1 inch thick. Cut the dough into 6 equal triangles.

Place the triangles of dough on the prepared pan and place in the oven on the bottom rack. Bake for 15 to 17 minutes, or until slightly browned and firm to the touch. Transfer to a wire rack to cool.

In a large bowl, crush 1 pint of the strawberries with a fork to make a sauce. Cut the remaining strawberries into slices and add to the bowl. Add 2 tablespoons of the confectioners' sugar, stir, and set aside.

(continued)

Using an electric mixer, whip the cream with the remaining 2 tablespoons confectioners' sugar and the Cointreau until soft peaks form. Be careful not to overwhip. Cover and refrigerate until ready to serve. Whisk a few times before using.

Using a serrated knife, cut each shortcake in half crosswise. Place bottom half on plate, spoon on strawberries, top with whipped cream and then cover with biscuit top. You might want to drizzle a small amount of strawberry juice over the top of the biscuit just for contrast, then sprinkle on remaining confectioners' sugar and serve.

A SOPHISTICATED SUPPER

Citron Vodka Martinis

Smoked Trout Canapés with Sour Cream and Chives

Provençal Beef Stew

Boiled New Potatoes Tossed in Parsley and Butter

Key Lime Pie

MENU MANAGER

1 day before dinner:	Prepare beef stew
Morning of dinner:	Prepare Key lime pie
1 hour before dinner:	Prepare trout canapés
30 minutes before dinner:	Boil new potatoes
When guests arrive:	Prepare martinis
15 minutes before serving:	Reheat stew Reheat potatoes in oven

Citron Vodka Martinis

Flavored vodkas add a fun twist to classic drinks, particularly martinis. This recipe makes 2 drinks at a time so you can pour them for guests more easily.

SERVES 2

Ice cubes

3 ounces citron vodka

1 ounce dry vermouth

4 pimiento-stuffed green olives

Fill a cocktail shaker with ice and add the vodka and vermouth. Shake until very cold. Strain into 2 chilled martini glasses. Add 2 olives to each glass.

Smoked Trout Canapés with Sour Cream and Chives

Here's an elegant and refined hors d'oeuvre that can be put together in minutes. The shells may be made out of phyllo dough or pastry dough. Canapé shells are found at finer grocery stores around the country. Some need to be cooked, while others are ready to be filled. If smoked trout isn't available, use smoked salmon.

SERVES 6

12 to 18 canapé shells, preferably thin and crisp

½ cup sour cream

9 ounces smoked trout, pulled into bite-sized pieces (about 1 cup)

¼ cup coarsely chopped fresh chives

Arrange the canapé shells on a platter. Fill each shell with a small dollop of sour cream. Add a piece of smoked trout. Garnish with a few chives and serve.

Provençal Beef Stew

On a foggy, snowy, rainy, or chilly day, nothing is better than stew. It warms every inch of your body and makes you feel at home wherever you eat it. The key to any kind of stew is to cook it slowly, letting all the rich flavors meld. This one adds the classic Provençal flavors of orange, thyme, and olives.

SERVES 6

3 tablespoons olive oil

4 pounds stewing beef, cut into large chunks

2 leeks, white part only, well washed, trimmed, and coarsely chopped

2 yellow onions, halved and thickly sliced crosswise

4 garlic cloves, halved

4 carrots, peeled and cut into chunks

2 teaspoons minced fresh thyme

2 teaspoons grated orange zest

2 bay leaves

1 cup pitted oil-cured olives

1 bottle dry red wine

4 cups beef stock

Juice of 1 orange

1 cup water (optional)

Sea salt and freshly ground pepper to taste

3 tablespoons coarsely chopped fresh flat-leaf parsley for garnish

Boiled New Potatoes Tossed in Parsley and Butter (page 66) for serving

In a large Dutch oven, heat 2 tablespoons of the olive oil over medium heat. Add the beef in batches and brown the chunks on all sides. Using a slotted spoon, transfer each batch of the beef to a bowl.

Add the remaining 1 tablespoon olive oil to the pot. Add the leeks, onions, and garlic and sauté for 5 to 7 minutes, or until lightly golden. Add the carrots, thyme, orange zest, bay leaves, and olives and sauté for 2 to 3 minutes.

Return the meat to the pot and add the red wine. Cook over high heat, uncovered, for 15 minutes, then reduce the heat to a low simmer, cover, and cook for 1½ hours, stirring every 30 minutes.

(continued)

Add the stock and orange juice. Cover and continue cooking for 1½ to 2 hours longer (a total of 3 to 3½ hours), or until the meat is very tender. If the stew becomes too thick, add 1 cup of water to loosen the sauce.

Season with the salt and pepper. Sprinkle with the parsley and bring the pot to the table for serving. Accompany with the boiled potatoes.

Boiled New Potatoes Tossed in Parsley and Butter

What would beef stew be without potatoes? I like to boil the potatoes separately, mash them on my plate, then spoon the stew and all its rich juices over them.

SERVES 6

20 to 24 small new potatoes

5 tablespoons unsalted butter

1 cup minced fresh flat-leaf parsley

Sea salt and freshly ground pepper to taste

Put the potatoes in a large saucepan and add cold water to cover. Bring the water to a boil over high heat. Reduce the heat to medium and simmer the potatoes for 20 to 25 minutes, or until tender when pierced with a knife.

Drain the potatoes well. Empty into a large bowl. Add the butter and toss the potatoes. Add the parsley, salt, and pepper. Toss again to coat. Serve warm.

Key Lime Pie

This recipe was inspired by a pie I once tasted at a small bakery in Rehobeth Beach, Delaware. The tangy lime filling perfectly complements the sweet graham cracker crust; so perfectly, in fact, that the traditional whipped cream topping is hardly needed and should be offered on the side. Key limes are slightly smaller and more sour than the more common Persian limes, although either works fine. Persian limes are readily available in most supermarkets, while Key limes may sometimes be found in specialty produce markets.

MAKES ONE 9-INCH PIE; SERVES 6

CRUST:
12 whole graham crackers
 (2 squares each)

¼ cup granulated sugar

6 tablespoons unsalted butter,
 melted

FILLING:
5 egg yolks

1 (14-ounce) can sweetened
 condensed milk

½ cup fresh lime juice, or more
 to taste

WHIPPED CREAM:
1 cup heavy cream

1 tablespoon confectioners'
 sugar, sifted, or to taste

To prepare the crust: Preheat the oven to 350°F. Adjust an oven rack in the lower third of the oven.

Put the graham crackers in a resealable plastic bag; remove as much air as possible and seal the bag. Using a rolling pin, crush the crackers into very small pieces without pulverizing them completely.

In a medium bowl, combine the graham cracker crumbs and sugar. Mix well. Stir in the butter until blended.

Pour the mixture into a 9-inch pie pan and press the crumbs into an even layer on the bottom and up the sides of the pan.

Bake the pie shell for 8 to 10 minutes, or until lightly browned. Transfer to a wire rack and let cool completely.

To prepare the filling: Preheat the oven to 350°F, if necessary.

In a large bowl, beat the yolks with a whisk until blended. Whisk in the milk to blend thoroughly. Whisk in the lime juice until smooth. The mixture should taste tangy at this point; if not, add a bit more lime juice.

Pour the filling into the cooled pie shell and carefully place in the oven on the bottom rack. Bake for about 15 minutes, or until the filling is set. Transfer to a wire rack and let cool for 30 to 45 minutes. Refrigerate for up to 8 hours. Remove from the refrigerator 30 minutes before serving.

To prepare the whipped cream: In a deep bowl, whip the cream until soft peaks form. Whisk in the confectioners' sugar. Serve the whipped cream in a bowl on the side so your guests can help themselves.

DINNERS FOR EIGHT

A LARGE DINNER PARTY

WHEN YOU PLAN A DINNER FOR EIGHT, YOU'VE MOVED INTO THE large-dinner-party category. You can expect that there will be multiple conversations going on around the table, making it a little noisier and a bit more animated than smaller gatherings. As for spending time with each guest, that's rarely going to happen. This is a party, so just have fun and engage in the lively conversations going on around the table.

Roasts, gratins, whole fish, and one-pot meals are perfect choices for eight or more. Not only will you have plenty of food, but these dishes are simple to prepare. The recipes in this section include a prized roasted pork shoulder and a rich, aromatic tagine, as well as my favorite dessert in the book, a Prune and Almond Tart. Enjoy!

AN AUTUMN DINNER

Roasted Almonds with Sea Salt

Roasted Pork Shoulder with Herbal Rub and Fennel

Potato, Onion, and Tomato Gratin

Sautéed Spinach

Prune and Almond Tart

MENU MANAGER

24 to 36 hours before dinner:	Marinate pork shoulder
Morning of dinner:	Prepare prune almond tart
	Prepare gratin
	Prepare almonds with sea salt
3 hours before dinner:	Cook pork shoulder
30 minutes before dinner:	Cover gratin with aluminum foil and reheat
	Prepare sautéed spinach
15 minutes before dinner:	Remove foil from gratin and continue to heat

Roasted Almonds with Sea Salt

Make this little nosh for any size crowd. As the almonds roast (which seems to happen instantly), the house fills with a delicious buttery odor. And if they're not consumed in one night, they will keep beautifully in an airtight container for up to 2 weeks.

MAKES 5 CUPS

5 cups whole unblanched almonds

3 tablespoons olive oil

2 teaspoons sea salt

Preheat the oven to 375°F.

In a large bowl, combine all the ingredients. Toss until the nuts are coated with the olive oil and salt.

Spread the almonds on 2 baking sheets. Roast for 8 to 10 minutes, or until golden brown. Transfer to paper towels and let cool for 10 minutes.

Transfer the nuts to a decorative bowl and serve.

Roasted Pork Shoulder
with Herbal Rub and Fennel

This recipe is loosely based on Judy Rodgers's wonderful "mock porchetta" in *The Zuni Café Cookbook.* If you usually find pork dry and not too tasty, the shoulder roast is the cut for you. It's a little fattier and therefore less dry. The rub imparts a fragrant wild-herbal flavor that will keep your guests asking for more. Note: You will need to start this dish 24 to 36 hours before serving.

SERVES 8

Two 2½-pound boneless pork shoulder roasts (Boston butt)

HERBAL RUB:

4 teaspoons grated orange zest

2 tablespoons capers, coarsely chopped

8 cloves garlic, coarsely chopped

3 anchovies, coarsely chopped

5 teaspoons fennel seeds, slightly bruised

4 teaspoons minced fresh rosemary

18 to 20 fresh sage leaves, coarsely chopped

2 tablespoons freshly ground pepper

2 teaspoons sea salt

8 fennel bulbs, trimmed and halved lengthwise

2 tablespoons olive oil

2 teaspoons sea salt

½ cup water

Trim all but a 1/4-inch layer of fat from the surface of the pork roasts. Using your thumbs, open the roasts at the seams to allow the maximum amount of surface to be coated with the seasonings.

To prepare the rub: In a medium bowl, combine all the ingredients. Stir well to blend.

Rub the herbal mixture over the surfaces and pack it into the crannies of the pork roasts. Reshape each roast and tie each separately with 4 to 5 pieces of kitchen twine. Cover with plastic wrap and refrigerate for at least 24 hours or up to 36 hours. Remove from the refrigerator 30 minutes before cooking.

(continued)

Preheat the oven to 350°F. Arrange the roasts on a rack in a roasting pan, leaving at least 3 inches between the roasts and the sides of the pan.

Toss the fennel bulbs in the olive oil and salt. Arrange the fennel around the roasts in the bottom of the roasting pan.

Roast for 1¼ hours, then turn the roasts over. Roast 45 minutes longer, then add the water and loosen the fennel with a spatula so it doesn't stick to the pan. Roast another 15 minutes (a total of 2¼ hours), or until the roasts are well browned and an instant-read thermometer inserted in the center of a roast registers 185°F.

Transfer the roasts to a cutting board and cover loosely with aluminum foil. Let stand for 10 minutes. Cut into ½-inch-thick slices, transfer to a platter, and surround with the roasted fennel.

Potato, Onion, and Tomato Gratin

Layers of thinly sliced potatoes, tomatoes, and onions sprinkled with Parmesan cheese make for a rich and exceedingly flavorful dish that goes beautifully with any fish or meat, especially the preceding pork roast.

SERVES 8

3 pounds baking potatoes, peeled and thinly sliced

Sea salt and freshly ground pepper to taste

3 large yellow onions, thinly sliced

½ cup olive oil

2 pounds tomatoes, thinly sliced

1 cup freshly grated Parmesan cheese

Preheat the oven to 375°F. Coat the bottom and sides of a large oval glass or ceramic gratin dish with olive oil.

Arrange a layer of half the potatoes in the dish. Top with half the onions, then half the tomatoes. Sprinkle with the salt and pepper. Drizzle with ¼ cup of the olive oil. Sprinkle with half of the cheese. Repeat the process to use the remaining ingredients.

Bake for about 1¼ hours, or until golden and bubbly. Serve hot.

Sautéed Spinach

Easy, delicious, and foolproof, this is a perfect side dish for almost any entrée. And frozen spinach doesn't have the slightly metallic taste of cooked fresh spinach.

SERVES 8

3 (16-ounce) packages frozen chopped spinach

¼ cup cold water

5 tablespoons olive oil

1 large yellow onion, coarsely chopped

1 ½ teaspoons freshly grated nutmeg

Sea salt and freshly ground pepper to taste

Put the frozen spinach in a large nonaluminum saucepan. Add the water, cover, and cook over medium heat, breaking up the spinach every 2 to 3 minutes with a wooden spoon, for 7 to 10 minutes, or until heated through.

Empty the spinach into a sieve or colander and press with a wooden spoon to force as much of the excess water out of the greens as you can. Set aside.

In a large saucepan, heat 3 tablespoons of the olive oil over medium heat. Add the onion and sauté for 7 to 10 minutes, or until golden. Add the spinach, the remaining olive oil, the nutmeg, salt, and pepper. Cook, stirring constantly, for 2 to 3 minutes, or until heated through.

Transfer to a warmed platter or serving bowl and serve at once.

Prune and Almond Tart

If you've never been particularly passionate about prunes, wait until you try this classic French tart. In this recipe, inspired by one from Patricia Wells, the combination of the sweet prunes and almonds makes for a mouthwatering delight. Be sure to use a good strong tea for plumping the prunes, and try to find moist, flavorful prunes. This tart is best served the day it is made.

MAKES ONE 10½-INCH TART; SERVES 8

PASTRY:

1 to 1¼ cups all-purpose flour

7 tablespoons cold unsalted butter, cut into pieces

⅛ teaspoon salt

2 teaspoons granulated sugar

3 tablespoons ice water

FILLING:

2 cups hot brewed strong tea (Earl Grey or any other dark blend)

1 pound prunes, pitted

¼ cup unblanched almonds

1 large egg

¾ cup crème fraîche

4½ tablespoons granulated sugar

2½ tablespoons brandy

3 teaspoons confectioners' sugar for dusting

To prepare the pastry: In a food processor, combine 1 cup of the flour, the butter, salt, and sugar. Pulse until the mixture resembles coarse crumbs, 5 to 10 seconds but no longer. Add the ice water and pulse 8 to 10 times, or until the pastry just begins to hold together. Transfer the dough to a floured surface and flatten into a disk. (If the dough is too sticky, knead it briefly, adding up to 1/4 cup more flour 1 tablespoon at a time as needed to make a smooth dough.) Wrap in plastic wrap and refrigerate for at least 1 hour or up 24 hours.

On a lightly floured surface, roll the dough out to a 12-inch-diameter round. As you roll, lift up the edges and dust some flour underneath to keep the dough from sticking to the surface. Fit the dough into a 10½-inch false-bottomed tart pan. Trim the overhang, leaving about ¾ inch, then fold the overhang back into the pan, pressing gently along the sides to create double-thick sides. Refrigerate for at least 20 minutes or up to 1 hour.

Preheat the oven to 375°F.

Prick the bottom of the tart shell with a fork and line with aluminum foil, pressing into all the edges to avoid shrinkage while baking. Fill with pie weights or dried beans. Bake for about 20 minutes, or just until the pastry begins to brown along the edges. Remove the weights and foil and return shell to the oven for 8 to 10 minutes, or until lightly browned all over. Let cool on a wire rack for at least 20 minutes.

To prepare the filling: Pour the hot tea over the prunes in a large bowl and let stand for at least 1 hour, or until soft. (Depending on when you plan to fill the tart shell, you may want to soak the prunes before you begin making the pastry.)

Preheat the oven to 375°F.

In a food processor, grind the almonds to a fine powder. Add the egg, crème fraîche, sugar, and brandy. Process until smooth.

Drain the prunes and briefly run them under water to remove any tea leaves. Delicately pat them dry with paper towels. Arrange the prunes in concentric circles in the cooled tart shell in one layer. Pour the almond mixture evenly over the prunes.

Bake for about 45 minutes, or until the filling begins to set and the shell is nicely browned. Remove from the oven and let cool completely on a wire rack. Dust evenly with the confectioners' sugar and serve.

A NORTH AFRICAN FEAST

Marinated Olives

**Spinach, Fuyu Persimmon, and
Pine Nut Salad with Citrus Vinaigrette**

Chicken Tagine with Couscous

**Roasted Eggplant Smothered in
Olive Oil, Parsley, and Garlic**

Phyllo Nests with Honey and Walnuts

MENU MANAGER

2 days before dinner: Prepare olives

Morning of dinner: Prepare chicken tagine
Prepare citrus vinaigrette

2 hours before dinner: Prepare phyllo nests without filling
Toast walnuts

1 hour before dinner: Prepare roasted eggplant
Assemble salad without dressing

15 minutes before dinner: Reheat chicken tagine

10 minutes before dinner: Prepare couscous

5 minutes before dinner: Toss salad

After main course: Assemble desserts

Marinated Olives

Olives are staples in my house. Not only are they wonderful to have on hand for a snack, but they always come in handy when you're having guests. These olives (pictured on page 81) are even better when they've marinated for a day or two, so make a big jar and keep it in your refrigerator.

MAKES 1 CUP

1 cup mixed olives (such as dry-cured, picholine, Gaeta, Kalamata, niçoise)

¼ cup olive oil

½ lemon, thinly sliced

1 very small dried red pepper

2 tablespoons minced fresh rosemary

In a large jar, combine all the ingredients. Shake to blend. Serve immediately or refrigerate for up to 1 month. Serve at room temperature.

Spinach, Fuyu Persimmon, and Pine Nut Salad with Citrus Vinaigrette

Fuyu persimmons are wonderful in salad. They're light and delicate in taste, and their crisp texture adds another element to this first course. Look for these squat round persimmons in the markets in fall and winter; they should be firm, not soft to the touch.

SERVES 8

¼ cup pine nuts

2 bunches spinach, stemmed, well washed, and dried

5 firm Fuyu persimmons, peeled, halved, and thinly sliced

CITRUS VINAIGRETTE:

1 tablespoon grated orange zest

1 tablespoon minced shallot

Juice of 1 lemon

1 tablespoon white wine vinegar

6 tablespoons olive oil

Sea salt and freshly ground pepper to taste

Preheat the oven to 400°F.

Spread the pine nuts on a pie plate and toast in the oven for 3 to 5 minutes, or until golden brown. Remove from the oven and set aside.

In a medium salad bowl, combine the spinach, persimmons, and pine nuts.

To prepare the vinaigrette: In a small bowl, combine all the vinaigrette ingredients. Whisk until blended.

Pour the vinaigrette over the salad and toss until evenly coated.

Chicken Tagine with Couscous

After trying a number of tagines, this one is still my favorite. The exotic flavors of this dish may inspire one of your guests to perform a belly dance after dinner.

SERVES 8

1 cup slivered almonds

12 chicken thighs, skinned

4 tablespoons olive oil

3 yellow onions, thinly sliced

2 teaspoons ground turmeric

2 teaspoons minced fresh ginger

2 cups chicken stock

15 threads saffron

1 teaspoon ground cumin

2 cups pitted prunes

3 tablespoons honey

1½ teaspoons ground cinnamon

Sea salt and freshly ground pepper
  to taste

Juice of 2 lemons

Couscous (page 86) for serving

1 cup minced fresh cilantro

Preheat the oven to 400°F. Spread the almonds on a pie plate and toast in the oven for 3 to 4 minutes, or until golden brown. Remove from the oven and set aside.

Rinse the chicken thighs and pat dry with paper towels.

In a large Dutch oven or heavy flameproof casserole, heat 2 tablespoons of the olive oil over medium heat until almost smoking. Add the chicken, in batches if necessary, and brown on both sides, 3 to 4 minutes per batch. Using tongs, transfer to a plate.

Add the remaining 2 tablespoons olive oil to the pan. Add the onions and sauté for 2 to 3 minutes. Add the browned chicken, turmeric, ginger, stock, saffron, and cumin. Reduce the heat to medium-low and cook, uncovered, stirring occasionally, for 30 minutes.

Add the prunes, honey, and cinnamon. Cover and cook 25 minutes longer, or until the chicken is nearly falling off the bone. Season with the salt and pepper. Stir in the lemon juice.

(continued)

Skim the fat from the liquid. Serve over the couscous, sprinkled with the toasted almonds and cilantro.

COUSCOUS

This tiny pasta works beautifully with tagines. The miniscule pearls soak up the sauce but keep their slightly grainy texture.

SERVES 8

2 cups water

3 tablespoons unsalted butter

1 teaspoon sea salt

2 cups couscous

In a large saucepan, combine the water, butter, and salt. Bring to a boil. Remove from the heat and stir in the couscous. Cover the pan and let stand for 6 minutes, or until the liquid is absorbed.

Remove the lid and fluff the couscous with a fork. Serve warm.

Roasted Eggplant Smothered in Olive Oil, Parsley, and Garlic

This Mediterranean dish, though simple to prepare, is bold in flavor. If you decide to serve it with a different main course, you might want to add crumbled feta cheese and coarsely chopped tomatoes.

SERVES 8

2 eggplants, cut diagonally into ¼-inch-thick rounds

1 teaspoon sea salt

½ cup olive oil

⅔ cup coarsely chopped fresh flat-leaf parsley

6 cloves garlic, minced

Spread the eggplant rounds out on 2 large platters. Sprinkle them with the salt, cover with a layer of paper towels, and let stand for 30 minutes. Remove the paper towels and pat eggplant rounds dry with fresh paper towels.

Preheat the oven to 400°F. In a medium bowl, mix the olive oil, parsley, and garlic together. Place a single layer of eggplant rounds on 2 baking sheets. Using a basting brush, baste both sides of the eggplant with the oil mixture.

Bake for 10 to 12 minutes, or until browned on the bottom and crisp on the edges. Turn the eggplant over and cook 10 to 12 minutes longer, or until browned on the second side. Let cool and serve at room temperature.

Phyllo Nests with Honey and Walnuts

The key to working with phyllo is to keep it moist. Thaw the frozen phyllo in the refrigerator and keep it covered with a damp cloth as you work. If you're not a big fan of walnuts, feel free to substitute pistachios or almonds.

MAKES 8 INDIVIDUAL PASTRIES

½ cup (1 stick) unsalted butter

8 sheets thawed frozen phyllo dough

½ cup walnuts, chopped

½ cup honey

2 cups fresh raspberries (optional)

Preheat the oven to 425°F.

In a small saucepan, melt the butter over low heat, making sure it doesn't burn.

Working with one sheet of phyllo at a time, pick it up from the center (as you would a handkerchief). Begin twisting the phyllo as you set it down on a baking sheet to make a free-form nest 3 to 4 inches in diameter. Using a pastry brush, brush the nest liberally with the melted butter. Repeat with each of the remaining 7 sheets of phyllo.

Bake the phyllo for 15 minutes, or until crisp and golden. Remove from the oven and let cool.

In a small skillet over medium-low heat, toast the walnuts for about 7 minutes, stirring frequently, until fragrant and lightly toasted.

In a small saucepan, warm the honey over low heat.

To serve, place a nest in the center of each plate. Liberally drizzle each with warm honey and sprinkle with toasted walnuts, and raspberries, if using. Serve at once.

A COOLING
SUMMER SPREAD

Guacamole with Chips

Andalusian Gazpacho

Poached Salmon with Cucumber, Dill, and Watercress Sauce

Wild Rice, Pecan, and Dried Cranberry Salad

Creamy Blueberry Pie

MENU MANAGER

1 day before dinner:	Prepare Andalusian gazpacho Prepare wild rice salad
Morning of dinner:	Prepare blueberry pie
2 hours before dinner:	Prepare sauce for salmon
1½ hours before dinner:	Prepare court bouillon for salmon
45 minutes before dinner:	Prepare poached salmon
30 minutes before dinner:	Prepare guacamole
5 minutes before serving:	Ladle soup into bowls and garnish

Guacamole with Chips

Guacamole is part comfort food, part party food. I know that if the bowl is placed in front of me, I'll finish it before dinner is served. If you want to serve a vegetable along with your chips, try jicama sticks.

MAKES 4 CUPS

4 large very ripe avocados, peeled and pitted

3 tablespoons finely chopped red onion

2 tomatoes, coarsely chopped

1 small jalapeño chile, seeded and minced

Juice of 1 lime

¼ teaspoon cayenne pepper

3 tablespoons sour cream

½ cup chopped fresh cilantro

Sea salt to taste

Blue and yellow corn chips for serving

In a large bowl, mash the avocados until chunky-smooth. Add the onion, tomatoes, jalapeño, lime juice, and cayenne. Stir to blend. Stir in the sour cream, cilantro, and salt.

Transfer to a decorative bowl. Place on a plate or platter and surround with the tortilla chips.

Andalusian Gazpacho

Your guests will wonder what makes this soup so smooth and creamy, but I'll bet that none of them will guess the secret ingredient. Make sure to chill it for at least 1 hour before serving, or add an ice cube to each bowl.

SERVES 8

4 cloves garlic, sliced

2 red or yellow bell peppers, seeded, deribbed, and coarsely chopped

1 cucumber, peeled and coarsely chopped

¼ red onion, coarsely chopped

12 very ripe tomatoes, coarsely chopped

6-inch-long piece baguette, dried overnight or toasted

¾ cup olive oil

4½ tablespoons Spanish sherry vinegar

1½ teaspoons sea salt

2 cups ice water

8 avocado slices for garnish

½ cup chopped fresh cilantro for garnish

In a blender, combine the garlic, bell peppers, cucumber, onion, tomatoes, bread, olive oil, vinegar, and salt. Pulse until smooth.

Pour the soup into a large bowl. Add the water and stir. Cover and refrigerate for at least 1 hour, or up to 3 days.

Ladle the soup into 8 soup bowls. Garnish each with a slice of avocado and a sprinkle of cilantro.

Poached Salmon with Cucumber, Dill, and Watercress Sauce

Serving a whole fish or a large piece of salmon to your dinner guests is both festive and fun. Poaching the salmon in a flavorful court bouillon gives it added taste, and decorating the fish and platter makes for an impressive presentation.

SERVES 8

COURT BOUILLON:

Bouquet garni: 2 bay leaves, 6 sprigs fresh flat-leaf parsley, 1 sprig fresh thyme, 4 celery tops with leaves, and 12 peppercorns, bruised

1 bottle dry white wine

2 small carrots, peeled and chopped

2 small red onions, quartered

1 tablespoon sea salt

Juice of 1 lemon

8 cups water

1 (5- to 6-pound) whole salmon, or a 5- to 6-pound midsection chunk

4 cucumbers or 8 lemons, thinly sliced, curly endive, and radishes or cherry tomatoes for garnish (optional)

Cucumber, Dill, and Watercress sauce (page 95) for serving

To prepare the court bouillon: Make a bouquet garni by tying the herbs, celery, and peppercorns in a square of cheesecloth.

In a large saucepan, combine the wine, carrots, onions, salt, lemon juice, water, and bouquet garni. Bring to a simmer over medium-low heat and cook for 30 minutes. Remove from heat and let cool.

Rinse the fish and cut off the fins. Wrap the fish loosely in cheesecloth. Place in a large roasting pan or a fish poacher.

Pour the court bouillon over the fish to cover. If more liquid is needed, add water.

Place the pan over 2 stove-top burners turned to medium-low. Cover and cook the fish for 30 minutes.

Using 2 spatulas, carefully remove the fish from the pan. Place it on a

(continued)

plate and carefully remove the cheesecloth, slowly pulling it away from the skin of the fish.

Remove the skin. Using a dull knife, gently scrape the gray skin residue covering the pink flesh. Cut off the head and discard (if needed). Transfer the fish to a platter.

If desired, overlap the slices of cucumbers or lemons on the fish to resemble scales. Surround the fish with curly endive and decorate the platter with radishes or cherry tomatoes.

Serve the sauce alongside.

CUCUMBER, DILL, AND WATERCRESS SAUCE

MAKES ABOUT 4 CUPS

2 cucumbers, peeled, halved lengthwise, and thinly sliced

4 large red onions, finely chopped

½ cup packed coarsely chopped fresh dill

½ cup packed coarsely chopped fresh watercress leaves

2 cups sour cream

½ teaspoon sugar

1 tablespoon rice vinegar

2 tablespoons fresh lemon juice

Sea salt and freshly ground pepper to taste

In a large bowl, combine the cucumbers, onions, dill, and watercress. Add the remaining ingredients and stir until blended.

Wild Rice, Pecan, and Dried Cranberry Salad

A mixture of wild and white rice creates a chewy, nutty backdrop for the full-flavored ingredients in this salad. Make it a couple of hours or a day ahead, as it tastes even better after standing.

SERVES 8

6 ¼ cups water

1 teaspoon sea salt

1 cup long-grain white rice

1 cup wild rice

¾ cup pecans, coarsely chopped

1 cup coarsely chopped fresh mint

½ cup dried cranberries

5 tablespoons grated orange zest

DRESSING:

Juice of 1 lemon

2 teaspoons Dijon mustard

3 tablespoons balsamic vinegar

2 tablespoons fresh orange juice

¾ cup olive oil

Sea salt and freshly ground pepper to taste

In a medium saucepan, bring 2¼ cups of the water to a boil. Add ½ teaspoon of the salt, then stir in the white rice. Reduce heat to a simmer. Cover and cook for 20 minutes, or until tender. Set aside to cool. Meanwhile, in another medium saucepan, bring the remaining 4 cups water to a boil. Add the remaining ½ teaspoon salt and stir in the wild rice. Reduce heat to a simmer. Cover and cook for 45 to 50 minutes, or until tender. Drain, rinse, and let cool.

Preheat the oven to 375°F. Spread the pecans on a pie plate and toast in the oven for 4 to 5 minutes, or until golden brown. Remove from the oven and set aside.

In a large bowl, combine the white and wild rice. Add the mint, pecans, cranberries, and orange zest. Toss to blend thoroughly.

To prepare the dressing: In a small bowl, combine all the dressing ingredients and whisk to blend.

(continued)

Pour the dressing over the rice mixture and toss well to make sure that all the ingredients are coated.

Serve immediately, let stand at room temperature for up to 2 hours, or cover and refrigerate for up to 1 day. Bring to room temperature before serving.

Creamy Blueberry Pie

The key to this pie is finding the freshest blueberries possible. It's so good I've baked it for ninth-generation residents of Maine, and even they agreed it was superb. The crust is so easy you'll want to use it for all your fruit pies!

MAKES ONE 9-INCH PIE; SERVES 8

CRUST:
1½ cups all-purpose flour

1½ teaspoons granulated sugar

½ teaspoon salt

½ cup canola oil

3½ tablespoons milk

FILLING:
4 cups fresh blueberries

⅔ cup granulated sugar

¼ cup all-purpose flour

½ teaspoon ground cinnamon

Pinch of salt

⅓ cup milk

⅔ cup heavy cream

WHIPPED CREAM:
1 cup heavy cream

1 tablespoon confectioners'
   sugar sifted, or to taste

Preheat the oven to 400°F.

To prepare the crust: In a 9-inch pie pan, combine all the ingredients and stir with a fork until blended. Using your fingers, press the dough into the pan and all the way up the sides, making a smooth rim with your fingers. Use the fork to prick the bottom of the crust to prevent bubbling.

To prepare the filling: Rinse the berries in a colander and remove any soft ones. Spread them out on a towel to dry slightly, then pour them into the pastry shell.

In a medium bowl, combine the sugar, flour, cinnamon, and salt. Add the milk and cream and whisk until smooth. Pour the mixture over the berries.

Bake for 40 to 45 minutes, or until set. After 25 to 35 minutes, check to see if you need to cover the edges with aluminum foil to prevent them from getting too dark.

Let cool on a wire rack, then refrigerate for at least 2 hours, or until well chilled.

To prepare the whipped cream: In a deep bowl, whip the cream until soft peaks form. Gradually stir in the confectioners' sugar. Serve in a bowl on the side so your guests can help themselves.

DINNERS
FOR TEN TO TWELVE
A LARGE DINNER PARTY

NOW, YOU'RE HAVING A PARTY! EXPECT LOTS OF CHATTER AND

a slight bit of chaos; lots of wineglasses, several salt and pepper shakers circulating, bread baskets making their way around the table, and friends offering to clear and serve. The mixture of people is less important, since if someone doesn't have instant rapport with one person there are plenty of others to engage in conversation. Here again, roasts, one-pot meals, gratins, and casseroles are easy to make and to serve for a large group.

Each of the recipes in this chapter will serve up to twelve; for ten you'll likely have leftovers. The recipes include a Baked Three-Cheese Pasta with Pancetta, a simple chicken dish, and a roasted leg of lamb, plus some casserole-style desserts: Rice Pudding with Brandied Cherries, a buttery fruit crisp, and dark chocolate brownies served with coffee ice cream. And after dinner, who knows? You could be rolling up the carpets.

A WINTER FEAST

Arugula, Blood Orange, and Fennel Salad with Walnut Oil

Roasted Leg of Lamb with Mint Pesto

Broccoli Mash

Roasted Mixed New Potatoes

Rice Pudding with Brandied Cherries

MENU MANAGER

Day before dinner:	Prepare rice pudding
Morning of dinner:	Prepare salad dressing
2½ hours before dinner:	Remove leg of lamb from refrigerator Assemble salad, cover with plastic wrap, and refrigerate
2¼ hours before dinner:	Start roasting leg of lamb Prepare mint pesto
1 hour before dinner:	Prepare broccoli mash Prep roasted potatoes
45 minutes before dinner:	Start roasting new potatoes
20 minutes before dinner:	Let lamb stand for 15 minutes, then carve
5 minutes before dinner:	Reheat broccoli mash

Arugula, Blood Orange, and Fennel Salad with Walnut Oil

The flavors in this salad literally burst in your mouth. If you can't find blood oranges, which are in season from winter to early spring, use navel oranges or a sweet pink grapefruit.

SERVES 10 TO 12

2 pounds arugula, stemmed

4 blood oranges, peeled and sectioned

3 fennel bulbs, trimmed and cut into paper-thin disks

DRESSING:
2 cloves garlic, minced

Juice of 1 lemon

Juice of 1 orange

¼ cup olive oil

½ cup walnut oil

2 tablespoons coarsely chopped fresh tarragon

Sea salt and freshly ground pepper to taste

In a large bowl, combine the arugula, oranges, and fennel.

To make the dressing: In a medium bowl, combine the garlic, citrus juices, and oils. Whisk the dressing until it begins to thicken. Stir in the tarragon, salt, and pepper.

Toss the salad with the dressing and serve.

Roasted Leg of Lamb with Mint Pesto

Even the mention of the word lamb sends my husband into a gleeful dance. Since he's half Greek, lamb has always been his family's meat of choice. As far as he's concerned, rubbing lamb with mustard and herbs falls short of the classic Greek treatment: garlic, olive oil, and salt. The mint pesto with a little feta continues the Greek theme.

SERVES 10 TO 12

1 leg of lamb (6 to 7 pounds)

6 to 7 cloves garlic, slivered

¼ cup olive oil

Sea salt and freshly ground pepper

MINT PESTO:

3 unpeeled cloves garlic

¼ cup pine nuts

2½ cups coarsely chopped fresh mint

¾ cup olive oil

½ cup crumbled feta cheese

Preheat the oven to 400°F.

Using a sharp knife, make incisions in the lamb and insert a sliver of garlic in each one. Rub the lamb with the olive oil, then sprinkle with the salt and pepper.

Place the lamb in a roasting pan. Roast for 1½ to 1¾ hours (about 15 minutes per pound) for medium-rare, or until an instant-read thermometer inserted in thickest part of the roast and not touching bone registers 124°F.

While the lamb is roasting, prepare the mint pesto: In a pie pan, roast the garlic cloves in the oven for 15 minutes, or until soft and slightly golden. In another pie pan, toast the pine nuts in the oven for 7 to 10 minutes, or until golden.

(continued)

In a blender or food processor, combine the mint, roasted garlic, olive oil, toasted pine nuts, and feta cheese. Process until smooth and creamy.

Transfer the lamb to a cutting board and let rest for about 15 minutes.

Cut the lamb into slices and serve with a large spoonful of the mint pesto on the side.

Broccoli Mash

This recipe was inspired by Alice Waters' wonderful long-cooked broccoli. I made it so often for a while that my husband very pleasantly asked me if we could vary the menu a little. This is also great cold, spread on a piece of toasted baguette that's been drizzled with a little olive oil.

SERVES 10 TO 12

6 pounds broccoli

Cloves from 2 bulbs garlic, thinly sliced

4½ to 5 cups water

1 cup olive oil

6 anchovy fillets, coarsely chopped

Sea salt and freshly ground pepper to taste

Juice of 2 lemons

1 cup freshly grated Parmesan cheese

Peel the broccoli stems. Slice the broccoli stems and florets crosswise into ¼- to ⅛-inch slices. In a stockpot, combine the broccoli, garlic, 4½ cups of the water, the olive oil, the anchovy fillets, salt, and pepper.

Bring to a boil and reduce heat to a simmer. Cook, uncovered, for 40 minutes. Check to make sure there is still liquid, and if the liquid is low, add the remaining ½ cup water. Cook 15 minutes longer, or until soft. Mash the broccoli in the pan, leaving a few lumps here and there. Add the lemon juice and stir.

Place the mash on a warmed platter and sprinkle with the Parmesan cheese. Serve warm.

Roasted Mixed New Potatoes

While I have suggested new potatoes for this recipe, feel free to experiment with the many varieties of potatoes now widely available. Yukon Gold, blue, and fingerlings all have their own distinctive taste and texture.

SERVES 10 TO 12

6 pounds new potatoes

¼ cup olive oil

**6 tablespoons coarsely chopped
    fresh rosemary**

**Sea salt and freshly ground pepper
    to taste**

Preheat the oven to 400°F. In a large bowl, combine all the ingredients and toss to coat the potatoes.

Spread the potatoes in a large baking dish or onto a baking sheet. Roast for 45 minutes, or until the potatoes are crisp on the outside and tender when pierced with a knife.

Rice Pudding with Brandied Cherries

This simple rice pudding is just as tasty warm as it is slightly chilled. I like using dried sweet cherries, but feel free to substitute sour ones if you prefer. When making this rice pudding, frequent stirring is a must, so put on a good CD, grab yourself a cup of coffee (or a glass of wine if you're making it the night before), and give yourself over to the task.

SERVES 10 TO 12

1 cup dried cherries

1 tablespoon brandy

6 cups water

2 teaspoons salt

3 cups long-grain white rice

5 cups milk

2½ cups heavy cream

2½ cups half-and-half

1⅓ cups sugar

2½ teaspoons pure vanilla extract

2 teaspoons ground cinnamon, plus more for garnish

Grated zest of 2 lemons

Put the cherries in a small bowl and add water to cover. Let soak for 5 to 10 minutes, or until plump. Drain and pat dry with paper towels. Return to the bowl and add the brandy. Set aside.

In a medium saucepan, bring the water to a boil and add 1½ teaspoons of the salt. Stir in the rice and reduce the heat to a simmer. Cover and cook for 20 minutes. Remove from the heat and let stand for 5 minutes, or until the water is absorbed. Let cool.

In a large saucepan, combine the rice, milk, cream, half-and-half, remaining ½ teaspoon salt, and sugar. Bring to a simmer over medium heat, stirring constantly so the rice doesn't stick. Reduce the heat to a low simmer and continue cooking uncovered, stirring frequently, for another 35 to 40 minutes, or until the mixture thickens.

Remove from the heat. Stir in the vanilla, cinnamon, lemon zest, and cherries until blended. Garnish with the cinnamon if desired. Serve warm, or let cool, cover, and refrigerate for at least 1 hour or overnight.

A SIMPLE SUPPER

Bruschetta with Chopped Tomatoes, Parsley, and Basil

Chicken à la Mama

Chopped Escarole Salad with Grapefruit and Avocado

Dark Chocolate Brownies with Coffee Ice Cream

MENU MANAGER

Day before dinner:	Prepare Chicken à la Mama
Night before dinner:	Prepare coffee ice cream
Morning of dinner:	Prepare topping for bruschetta Prepare salad dressing Prepare chocolate brownies
1 hour before dinner:	Prepare salad without dressing; cover with plastic wrap and refrigerate
30 minutes before dinner:	Prepare toasts for bruschetta Reheat Chicken à la Mama
5 minutes before dinner:	Assemble toasts for bruschetta

Bruschetta with Chopped Tomatoes, Parsley, and Basil

This classic Italian favorite (pictured on page 111) is best when all the ingredients are fresh. Try to find the best bread available, and don't skimp on the tomatoes since they are the crucial ingredient. I suggest cherry tomatoes here as they often have more flavor, but feel free to substitute other flavorful vine-ripened tomatoes.

SERVES 10 TO 12

4 cloves garlic, 2 minced and 2 whole

3 cups cherry tomatoes, chopped

¼ cup olive oil

2 tablespoons coarsely chopped fresh flat-leaf parsley

¼ cup coarsely chopped fresh basil

½ teaspoon sea salt

1 tablespoon capers, minced

1 loaf ciabatta bread, cut into thick slices

Preheat the oven to 400°F.

In a medium bowl, combine the minced garlic, tomatoes, olive oil, parsley, basil, salt, and capers. Mash the ingredients together.

Place the bread on a baking sheet and toast for 5 minutes on each side, or until golden.

Rub the toasts with the whole garlic cloves. Cut the toasts in half. Spread 1 tablespoonful of the mixture on each garlic toast.

Put the toasts on a decorative platter and serve.

Chicken à la Mama

It could be French, it could be Italian, and it could become your favorite chicken recipe. This Mediterranean-inspired chicken dish is pure, heartwarming comfort food. I like it best served over plain egg noodles.

SERVES 10 TO 12

1 tablespoon unsalted butter

3 tablespoons olive oil

4 leeks, white part only, trimmed, well washed, and finely chopped

5 shallots, minced

14 shiitake mushrooms, stemmed and cut into ¼-inch-thick slices

25 cremini mushrooms, quartered

10 chicken breast halves

5 chicken thighs

½ cup all-purpose flour

Sea salt and freshly ground pepper to taste

1½ cups dry white wine

10 ounces frozen artichoke hearts

6 anchovy fillets, coarscly chopped

2 bay leaves

About 1 cup water

¼ cup fresh lemon juice

1 cup coarsely chopped fresh flat-leaf parsley

In a large Dutch oven or heavy flameproof casserole, melt the butter with 1 tablespoon of the olive oil. Add the leeks and shallots and sauté over medium heat for 5 to 7 minutes, or until soft. Add the mushrooms and sauté until limp. Using a slotted spoon, transfer the vegetables to a bowl.

Rinse the chicken pieces and dry them with paper towels. Put the flour on a large plate and season with the salt and pepper. Dredge the chicken breasts and thighs evenly in the flour.

Add the remaining 2 tablespoons olive oil to the same pan and heat over medium-low heat. Brown the chicken on all sides, about 8 minutes.

Stir in the leeks, shallots, and mushrooms, then add the wine. Stir in the artichokes, anchovy fillets, and bay leaves.

Cover and cook for 1½ to 1¾ hours, or until the chicken is beginning to fall off the bone. Check after 45 minutes and add the water as necessary to keep the chicken moist.

(continued)

Pull the skin off the chicken with a fork and discard the skin. Stir the casserole, pulling some of the chicken meat off the bones. Add the lemon juice, and season with the salt and pepper. Sprinkle with the parsley and serve.

Chopped Escarole Salad with Grapefruit and Avocado

The bitter crunch of the escarole works well with the soft texture of the avocado and slightly sweet, slightly tart taste of the grapefruit.

SERVES 10 TO 12

Leaves from 2 heads escarole, torn into bite-sized pieces

2 Ruby Red grapefruits, peeled, seeded, and cut into bite-sized chunks

2 avocados, peeled, pitted, and cut into bite-sized chunks

½ red onion, thinly sliced

DRESSING:

1 ½ tablespoons Dijon mustard

Pinch of sugar

¾ cup olive oil

3 tablespoons cider vinegar

¼ cup fresh grapefruit juice

Sea salt and freshly ground pepper to taste

In a large salad bowl, combine the escarole, grapefruits, avocados, and onion.

To prepare the dressing: In a small bowl, combine all the dressing ingredients. Whisk until fully blended.

Pour the dressing over the salad and toss. Serve immediately.

Dark Chocolate Brownies
with Coffee Ice Cream

I've never described myself as a chocolate lover, but these rich, chewy brownies based on Robert Morocco's recipe in *The Baker's Dozen* could someday make me join the camp. I like to serve these with coffee ice cream, but they are delicious all by themselves as well.

MAKES 1 QUART ICE CREAM AND 12 BROWNIES

COFFEE ICE CREAM:

2 ½ cups milk

1 ½ cups sugar

2 eggs, well beaten

½ cup cold espresso

½ teaspoon salt

1 cup heavy cream

DARK CHOCOLATE BROWNIES:

¾ cup coarsely chopped walnuts

5 ounces semisweet chocolate, chopped

2 ounces unsweetened chocolate, chopped

½ cup (1 stick) unsalted butter, cut into pieces

½ teaspoon salt

1 cup sugar

1 ½ teaspoons pure vanilla extract

2 large eggs at room temperature

7 tablespoons all-purpose flour

To prepare the ice cream: In a medium saucepan, heat the milk over low heat until bubbles form around the edges of the pan. Add the sugar and stir until dissolved. Remove from heat and let cool for 10 minutes.

In a small stainless-steel bowl, combine the milk mixture and beaten eggs. Set the bowl over a saucepan of barely simmering water. Cook, stirring constantly, for 10 to 12 minutes, or until the mixture is thick enough to coat the back of the spoon. Remove from the heat and let cool.

Cover and refrigerate for at least 1 hour. Stir in the coffee, salt, and cream. Refrigerate for 1 more hour. Freeze in an ice cream maker according to the manufacturer's instructions.

(continued)

To prepare the brownies: Preheat the oven to 325°F. Adjust an oven rack in the lower third of the oven. Butter an 8- or 9-inch square baking pan. Line the bottom of the pan with aluminum foil, allowing the extra to hang over the sides.

Spread the walnuts on a baking sheet and bake for 10 to 12 minutes, or until toasted and fragrant. Remove from the oven and let cool.

In a double boiler over barely simmering water, melt the chocolates and butter. Remove from heat and let cool for about 10 minutes.

Stir in the salt, sugar, and vanilla until well blended. Whisk in the eggs one at a time. Stir in the flour until well blended. Stir in the walnuts.

Spread in the prepared pan and bake for about 35 minutes, or until a toothpick inserted in the center comes out clean. The top should be puffy and shiny and cracked. Remove from the oven and let cool in the pan for 1 hour.

Lift the cake from the pan using the foil and invert onto a plate. Carefully remove the foil and turn the cake right-side up. Using a sharp knife, cut into 10 or 12 equal brownies.

To serve, place a brownie on each of 10 or 12 plates and top with a scoop of ice cream.

COMFORT FOOD FOR FRIENDS

Bagna Cauda with Fennel, Endives, and Cauliflower

Baked Three-Cheese Pasta with Pancetta

Frisée Salad with Mushrooms, Tomatoes, and Red Onion

Apricot, Cherry, and Blueberry Crisp with Vanilla Bean Ice Cream

MENU MANAGER

Night before dinner:	Prepare three-cheese pasta
	Prepare vanilla bean ice cream
Morning of dinner:	Prepare fruit crisp
1 hour before dinner:	Prepare dipping sauce
	Prepare crudités and toss with lemon juice
30 minutes before dinner:	Prepare salad
	Prepare salad dressing
25 minutes before dinner:	Reheat baked pasta
Just before dinner:	Toss salad with dressing
	Reheat fruit crisp

Bagna Cauda with Fennel, Endives, and Cauliflower

This classic dip from the Piedmont region of Italy is served warm—the name means "hot bath." It traditionally accompanies raw vegetables, but it's also good with a crusty Italian bread.

SERVES 10 TO 12

1 cup olive oil

12 garlic cloves, thinly sliced

20 to 25 oil-packed anchovies, chopped

¾ cup (1½ sticks) unsalted butter, cut into large chunks

¼ cup coarsely chopped fresh flat-leaf parsley

4 large fennel bulbs, trimmed and quartered

Leaves from 6 to 8 Belgian endives

1 large cauliflower, cut into florets

In a small saucepan, heat the olive oil over low heat. Add the garlic and anchovies and cook for 3 to 4 minutes. Add the butter and melt. Stir to break up the garlic and anchovies. Cook 2 to 3 minutes longer.

Pour into a large bowl and whisk until blended. Pour into a fondue pot and light the heat beneath it. Sprinkle with parsley. Serve the vegetables on a platter next to the bagna cauda.

Baked Three-Cheese Pasta with Pancetta

This sophisticated version of macaroni and cheese is slightly dressed-up comfort food at its best.

SERVES 10 TO 12

3 tablespoons, plus ½ cup (1 stick) unsalted butter

1½ large yellow onions, finely chopped

1 pound pancetta, cut into pea-sized cubes

½ cup all-purpose flour

3½ cups half-and-half

2 teaspoons sea salt

½ teaspoon freshly ground pepper

4 cups (1 pound), plus 3 tablespoons freshly grated Parmesan cheese

2 pounds penne pasta

1 cup shredded Gruyère cheese

1 cup shredded fontina cheese

½ cup dried bread crumbs

2 tablespoons minced fresh flat-leaf parsley

In a medium saucepan, melt the 3 tablespoons butter over low heat. Add the onions and sauté for 5 to 7 minutes, or until lightly golden and soft. Add the pancetta and sauté for 10 to 12 minutes, or until lightly browned. Remove from the heat and set aside.

Preheat the oven to 375°F. Butter two 3-quart baking dishes.

In a large saucepan, melt the ½ cup butter over medium-low heat. Add the flour and stir constantly for 3 minutes; do not brown. Whisk in the half-and-half and cook, whisking occasionally, until thickened, about 5 minutes. Remove from the heat, stir in the salt, pepper, and the 4 cups Parmesan cheese until the cheese is melted.

In a large pot of salted boiling water, cook the penne until tender but firm, about 12 minutes. Drain and toss with the cheese sauce. Add the pancetta mixture and toss thoroughly. Set aside.

In a medium bowl, combine the Gruyère and fontina. Stir to blend.

In a small bowl, combine the 3 tablespoons Parmesan cheese, the bread crumbs, and parsley.

(continued)

Layer one-fourth of the pasta in each baking dish. Sprinkle each layer evenly with one-fourth of the cheese mixture. Repeat the process with the remaining pasta and cheese mixture. Cover the top with the bread crumb mixture.

Bake for 35 to 45 minutes, or until golden brown. Remove from the oven and let rest for 5 minutes before serving. If you are planning on reheating, bake the pasta for 25 to 30 minutes initially, then reheat for 10 to 15 minutes.

Frisée Salad with Mushrooms, Tomatoes, and Red Onion

This simple yet sophisticated salad is full of color and flavor. Make sure to slice the onion thinly so it doesn't overpower the salad.

SERVES 10 TO 12

Leaves from 6 small heads frisée, torn in half

20 white mushrooms, thinly sliced

1 cup small cherry tomatoes

½ red onion, very thinly sliced

DRESSING:

¾ cup olive oil

1 teaspoon honey

2½ tablespoons red wine vinegar

2½ tablespoons fresh lemon juice

¼ cup whole plain yogurt

½ teaspoon herbes de Provence

Sea salt and freshly ground pepper to taste

In a large salad bowl, combine the frisée, mushrooms, tomatoes, and onion.

To prepare the dressing: In a medium bowl, combine the olive oil and honey, whisking until smooth. Whisk in the vinegar and lemon juice. Gradually whisk in the yogurt, herbs, salt, and pepper. Whisk for 1 to 2 minutes, or until creamy.

Pour the dressing over the salad and toss. Serve immediately.

Apricot, Cherry, and Blueberry Crisp with Vanilla Bean Ice Cream

This classic American crisp works best with the freshest fruits you can find, and is easily prepared earlier in the day and reheated just before serving. Feel free to experiment with different fruits; the topping works well with just about any combination.

SERVES 10 TO 12

FILLING:

3 pounds fresh apricots, peeled, pitted, and cut into ½-inch-thick slices

2 pounds fresh sweet cherries, pitted

2 cups fresh or frozen blueberries

1½ cups granulated sugar

½ cup all-purpose flour

TOPPING:

2½ cups old-fashioned oats

1½ cups all-purpose flour

1½ cups packed dark brown sugar

2 teaspoons ground cinnamon

2 teaspoons salt

1 cup (2 sticks) unsalted butter, melted

Vanilla Bean Ice Cream (page 22)

Preheat the oven to 400°F. Butter a 9-by-13-inch baking dish.

To prepare the filling: In a large bowl, combine the apricots, cherries, blueberries, sugar, and flour. Pour the mixture into the prepared dish.

To prepare the topping: In a separate large bowl, combine the oats, flour, brown sugar, cinnamon, and salt. Mix thoroughly. Add the melted butter and stir until blended. Sprinkle the topping evenly over the fruit mixture.

Bake for 25 to 30 minutes, or until the topping is brown and the fruit bubbles. Let cool for 5 to 10 minutes before serving. If made ahead, reheat in a preheated 350°F oven for 10 to 15 minutes. Serve with the vanilla ice cream.

INDEX

TABLE OF EQUIVALENTS

The exact equivalents in the following tables have been rounded for convenience.

LIQUID/DRY MEASURES

U.S.	METRIC
¼ teaspoon	1.25 milliliters
½ teaspoon	2.5 milliliters
1 teaspoon	5 milliliters
1 tablespoon (3 teaspoons)	15 milliliters
1 fluid ounce (2 tablespoons)	30 milliliters
¼ cup	60 milliliters
⅓ cup	80 milliliters
½ cup	120 milliliters
1 cup	240 milliliters
1 pint (2 cups)	480 milliliters
1 quart (4 cups, 32 ounces)	960 milliliters
1 gallon (4 quarts)	3.84 liters
1 ounce (by weight)	28 grams
1 pound	454 grams
2.2 pounds	1 kilogram

OVEN TEMPERATURE

FAHRENHEIT	CELSIUS	GAS
250	120	½
275	140	1
300	150	2
325	160	3
350	180	4
375	190	5
400	200	6
425	220	7
450	230	8
475	240	9
500	260	10

LENGTH

U.S.	METRIC
⅛ inch	3 millimeters
¼ inch	6 millimeters
½ inch	12 millimeters
1 inch	2.5 centimeters